WORLD OF SPORTS

BICYCLING

Published by Smart Apple Media
123 South Broad Street, Mankato, Minnesota 56001

Photography: pages 7, 8—CORBIS/Bettmann;
page 14—CORBIS/Stephanie Maze; page 16—CORBIS/Sean
Sexton Collection; pages 19, 24—CORBIS/Todd Gipstein

Design and Production by EvansDay Design

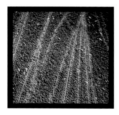

LIBRARY OF CONGRESS CATALOGING-IN-PUBLICATION DATA

Bach, Julie S., 1963–
Bicycling / by Julie Bach.
p. cm. — (World of sports)
Includes index.
Summary: Details the history, equipment, techniques, and
competitions of bicycling.
ISBN 1-887068-53-8
1. Cycling—Juvenile literature. [1. Bicycles and bicycling.]
I. Title. II. Series: World of sports (Mankato, Minn.)
GV1043.5.B33   1999
796.6'2—dc21   98-33682

9 8 7 6 5 4 3 2

BICYCLING

JULIE BACH

I love the bicycle. I always have.
I can think of no sincere, decent
human being, male or female,
young or old, saintly or sinful,
who can resist the bicycle.

William Saroyan

Two-wheeled Champions

■

TODAY HE LIVES a quiet life in Minnesota. But for almost a decade,

Greg LeMond was the most heroic figure in bicycling. To many, he still

is. Handsome, friendly, and dedicated to racing, LeMond won the leg-

endary Tour de France three times—in 1986, 1989, and 1990. He suffered

setbacks, injuries, and even a near-fatal hunting

accident, but he never gave up on the sport he loved.

Eddy Merckx, the greatest road cyclist in history, won 525 of the 1,800 races he entered.

Bicycle racing is a demanding sport that requires

fitness, stamina, and strategy. No bicycle race is more demanding than

the Tour de France. Although the route changes every year, each race

covers between 2,500 and 3,000 miles (4,023–4,827 km). The rider who

wins this prestigious event is considered the best cyclist in the world.

LeMond first won the race in 1986. He probably would have won it in

1987, too, but that winter he was shot in a hunting accident and barely

survived. Fans thought he would never race again, but LeMond made

an amazing comeback. In 1989, he won the Tour de France by eight sec-

onds—the closest finish in the history of the race.

Despite the rigors of riding and training, LeMond loved racing. In 1987, he wrote, "There are many times I wish I was playing 18 holes of golf instead of training in miserable cold weather. But in the final analysis, I'd rather win the Tour de France than play 18 holes of golf. That's why I do it."

Judging by his cycling success, Miguel Indurain probably feels the same way. He won the Tour de France every year from 1991 to 1995, an accomplishment that no other racer has achieved. Indurain's relentless racing style and high tolerance for pain earned him the nickname "The Machine."

One of today's brightest cycling stars is Lance Armstrong, who, in the early 1990s, became the second-youngest person ever to win a world road championship. In 1996, though,

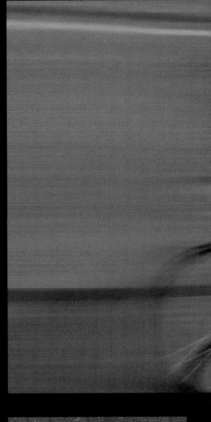

BICYCLIST GREG LEMOND (LEFT) ESTABLISHED HIMSELF AS ONE OF THE WORLD'S GREATEST ROAD RACERS BY WINNING THE TOUR DE FRANCE THREE TIMES.

THE THIN TIRES AND SLEEK BUILD OF TOURING BIKES MAKE THEM THE FASTEST BICYCLES ON PAVED SURFACES.

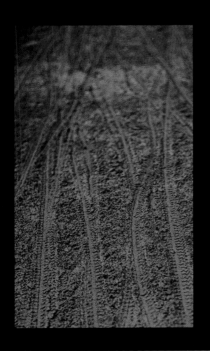

Armstrong was diagnosed with cancer and given just a 10 percent chance of living. Armstrong not only survived, but he came back to win the Tour de France in 1999. "It's a great honor," he said after crossing the finish line in Paris, "for American cycling and for the cancer community."

Although road racing has always been the most popular bicycle competition, mountain biking has surged in popularity in the last decade. Southern California and Boulder, Colorado, are two hot spots for mountain biking. The trails in these areas are steep, and the competition is stiff.

In the early 1980s, Jock Boyer became the first American to race in the Tour de France. Boyer paved the way for other top American racers such as Greg LeMond.

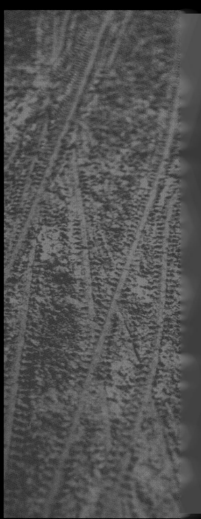

One of the world's best **mountain bike** racers is Paola Pezzo, an Italian woman who won the 1997 **cross-country** world championship. In 1996, Pezzo won a gold medal in the same event at the Olympics. During the Olympic race, Pezzo crashed. Although she knew she was probably out of the running, Pezzo got back on her bike. Riding hard, she gained a solid lead over the other riders. "It wasn't quite a miracle," she said, "but it almost seemed like one to me."

Pezzo follows in the footsteps of Juli Furtado, who may have been the greatest mountain bike competitor

Beryl Burton brought increased respect to women's racing with her determination, talent, and ability to win against men. In 1967, she became the first woman to break a man's record, riding 277.25 miles (446 km) in a 12-hour time trial.

mountain bike *a bicycle designed for use on hills and rough surfaces*

cross-country *a type of bicycle race that covers long distances and many types of terrain*

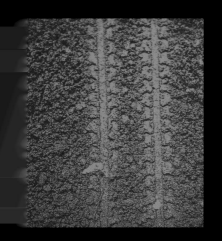

of all time. Between 1991 and 1995, Furtado won more championships than any other rider. In November 1997, lupus—a disease that attacks the joints, skin, and heart—forced her to announce her retirement.

Most bicycle racers are as familiar with tragedy as they are with victory. But riders would not stick with it if they didn't love competition. Laurent Brochard, the 1997 world road racing champion, put it this way: "I race . . . to confront others and do the best with the talent I have."

The Early Years

—

THE PURSUIT OF racing victories isn't the only reason that people ride bicycles. Some ride for fun, while others pedal for fitness. Many adults and children commute to work or school by bicycle.

No one knows exactly when the first bicycle was built. Egyptian **hieroglyphics** from as long ago as 3000 B.C. show human figures riding on a long pole connecting two wheels. Ancient Roman paintings from about 2,000 years later show men in togas on two-wheelers. These pictures, however, are not accompanied by written records.

In 1899, Major Taylor became the first African-American world champion in any American sport. He was cycling's biggest star at the turn of the century, earning more money for a single appearance than baseball's Ty Cobb made in a whole season.

The first bicycle design may have come from Élie Richard, a French woodworker who drafted plans for a two-wheeled vehicle. Richard apparently never built anything from these plans, but another Frenchman did. In 1693, Jacques Ozanam used Richard's plan to build a rough model of a vehicle that looked somewhat like a modern-day bike.

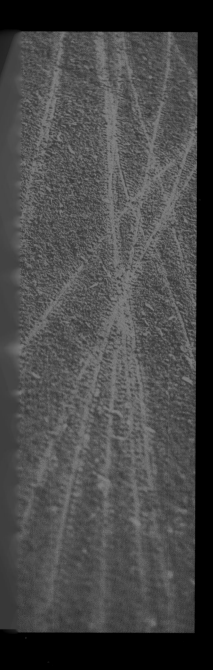

hieroglyphics *a form of pic-
ture writing used by the ancient
Egyptians*

Unfortunately, no one was very interested in Ozanam's contraption. Almost 100 years passed before the *Journal de Paris* reported that two men had built a machine called a *vélocipède*. The new word combined the Latin terms *velox*, or "speed," and *ped*, or "foot."

Despite its name, the vélocipède wasn't very speedy. It had no pedals or cranks, and riders couldn't turn the front wheel from side to side. They simply pushed themselves along the ground with their feet, then coasted.

Nevertheless, the heavy, wooden vélocipèdes were a hit in Paris during the 1790s. Wealthy young men pushed their vélocipèdes about the streets, scattering pedestrians and raising a ruckus. Although fashionable, the vehicles were cumbersome and impossible to steer.

In 1880, bicyclists formed the League of American Wheelmen, the first governing body for bicycling in the United States. It was later renamed the League of American Bicyclists.

In 1818, a German nobleman named Baron Karl Von Drais de Sauerbrun invented a bicycle with handlebars and a front wheel that moved from side to side. In a demonstration of the new bicycle in Paris, riders rode in circles around the fountains at Luxembourg Gardens.

The problem of steering had been solved, but the problem of weight remained. Dennis Johnson, a London blacksmith, came up with a solution in 1819. Johnson built a bicycle frame using thin iron rods instead of heavy pieces of wood. He called his contraption a "hobby horse."

Progress had been made in bicycle designs, but riders were still pushing themselves along the ground with their feet. As a result, they generally were not able to move very fast. This final problem was solved by Pierre Michaux, a Paris blacksmith and coach builder who added pedals to an old vélocipède in 1861. Soon, other builders began copying Michaux's invention, and Paris became the center of the new bicycling industry.

It was inevitable that human beings on wheels would eventually challenge each other to races. In 1868, Michaux's company organized a 3,937-foot (1,200 m) race on the out-

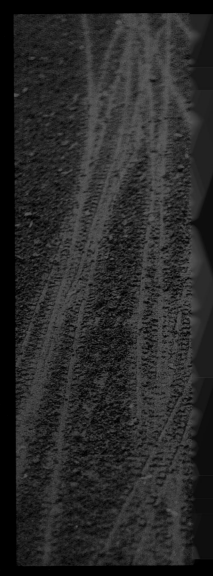

EARLY IN ITS DEVELOPMENT, SOME FORMS OF THE BICYCLE WERE PRACTICALLY ALL WHEEL WITH LITTLE FRAME.

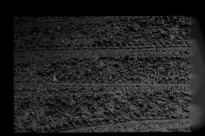

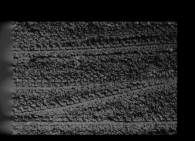

skirts of Paris. The winner, a young Eng-lishman named James Moore, won a prize of 600 francs. That September, a bicycling magazine sponsored the first *In 1972, Eddy Merckx set a world record by biking 30.65 miles (49.3 km) in just one hour. His record stood for the next 12 years.* endurance race, which followed a course from Paris to Rouen. Two hundred riders covered 83 grueling miles (133.5 km) over cobblestone and dirt roads. James Moore won again, partly because he was the first rider to use rubber tires instead of wooden ones.

Evolution of the Bicycle

OVER THE YEARS, manufacturers built many kinds of bicycles, and people were eager to try them all. By the early part of the 20th century, the sport of bicycle riding was second in popularity only to baseball.

Around World War II, many adults started riding motorcycles. Soon afterward, bicycle manufacturers had an idea. Kids loved their bicycles, but many wanted to ride motorcycles. When manufacturers began working on designs that were a cross between bicycles and motorcycles, the **BMX** bike was born.

During the 1995 Tour de France, Fabio Casartelli— the 1992 Olympic road race gold medalist—crashed without a helmet and died. The next day, all of the riders rode together slowly and let Casartelli's teammates win that stage of the race.

BMX is short for "bicycle motocross." BMX bikes have small tires that are thick and knobby, resembling motorcycle tires. The bikes have a single gear, brake levers on the handlebars, and motorcycle-style seats. BMX bikes weigh between 20 and 30 pounds (9–13.6 kg) and are sturdy enough to take a beating from young riders.

Mountain bikes were born in the early 1970s in Marin County, California. At that time, a group of riders dreamed of a better way to ride up

and down the steep trails north of San Francisco. These daring riders included Gary Fisher, Charlie Kelly, Joe Breeze, Tom Ritchey, and Wende Cragg. They wanted a bike that could handle "Repack Hill," a hill so steep that bicycle riders had to repack the grease on their **coaster brakes** every time they reached the bottom.

The Marin County riders noticed how easily BMX bikes could cover such treacherous terrain. The group started experimenting with new bicycle designs, adding rugged tires and stronger wheel rims to the lightweight frames of road bikes so they could better handle bumps and shocks. The riders added new **handbrakes** for stopping power on steep hills, straightened the handlebars, and replaced the single gear of the BMX bike with multiple gears—a feature that gave them far more flexibility and speed for riding on hills.

BMX *stands for "bicycle motocross"; BMX bikes are tough, all-terrain bikes made for smaller riders*

coaster brakes *bicycle brakes applied by pedaling backward*

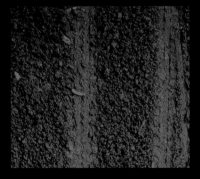

THE RUGGED SPORT OF BMX RACING DEMANDS THAT RIDERS WEAR HELMETS, GLOVES, AND PROTECTIVE PADDING.

handbrakes *bicycle brakes applied by squeezing a lever on the handlebars*

touring bikes *strong but lightweight bikes designed for travel on paved roads*

centuries *bicycle races that cover 100 miles (161 km)*

ten-speed *a bicycle that has 10 gear settings*

The new mountain bikes, also known as all-terrain bikes or off-road bikes, were a hit. By the 1980s, mountain bikes were available throughout the United States. By 1996, mountain bike racing had become an exhibition sport at the Summer Olympic Games.

Mountain bikes work well for trail riding. They've also become popular with urban commuters and delivery workers who have to ride over and around obstacles on city streets and sidewalks. However, the most popular bikes sold around the world today are called **touring bikes**.

As early as 1870, bicycle riders began forming groups to tour the countryside. These tours were called **centuries**, because the rides were 100 miles (161 km) long. Bicyclists still train to ride centuries today.

When Lance Armstrong won a stage of the 1995 Tour de France after Fabio Casartelli's untimely death, he crossed the finish line pointing at the sky. "I rode with the strength of two men today," he said.

By the 1950s, riders were cycling on a bike called the English racer or the middleweight. It was a light bike with narrow tires, three gears, and brakes on both wheels. The English racer evolved into the **ten-speed**, which was the forerunner of today's touring bikes.

Touring bikes have small, hard seats and thin, hard tires. The handlebars curve downward, and the grips are low. These bikes, designed for riding on paved roads, are strong but lightweight and have as many as 18 gears. Bicyclists use them for both recreation and racing.

Guts and Glory

CYCLISTS CAN COMPETE in BMX racing, mountain biking, or road racing. BMX racing is a great way for kids to get started in bicycling competition. Most racers are between 8 and 16 years old. The sport is especially popular in southern California, where there are many tracks and competitions. "Kids love to ride, and it's easier to teach them how to do it," one BMX race organizer said. "You can't teach adults how to ride bikes—how to race—like you can a kid."

BMX races are short, fast, and exciting. They are run on dirt tracks about 1,000 feet (305 m) long, and each race generally lasts 35 to 45 seconds. A carnival-like atmosphere surrounds the riders as they warm up on their bikes and as parents and siblings cheer them on. BMX racing emphasizes good sportsmanship, safety, and family involvement. There are many benefits to the racing experience. "You get these kids on bikes in competitive situations at such an early age, and they learn so much," said one BMX

Marco Pantani won the 1998 yellow jersey, becoming the first Italian to win the Tour de France in 33 years. His team members dyed their hair platinum blonde on the final day of the tour; since Pantani didn't have hair, he dyed his goatee instead.

fan. "Not just bike handling, but how to handle themselves in a pack of riders and how to behave in competition."

BMX races require skill and speed. The best riders combine strength and courage with a willingness to take risks. They fly over jumps and skid over challenging obstacles. When the weather is good, the tracks can be fast and hard; if it's raining, the riders get covered with mud as they slip and slide around turns. Racers take plenty of spills, so they wear helmets, knee pads, elbow pads, and other protective gear.

Cyclist Andy Hampsten is the only American to have won the grueling race called Giro d'Italia. He rode over a high mountain pass in a blinding snowstorm to claim the pink jersey.

The most important BMX competition of the year is the Red Zinger Mini-Classic, which is held near Boulder, Colorado. It attracts more competitors than any other race.

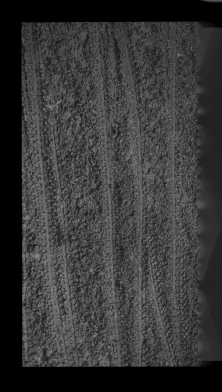

PERFORMING AERIAL STUNTS ON SPECIALLY DESIGNED RAMPS HAS BECOME A POPULAR FORM OF BMX COMPETITION.

Wild Ones

THE THICK TIRES AND STURDY FRAMES OF ALL-TERRAIN BIKES ALLOW TODAY'S CYCLISTS TO STRAY FAR FROM THE BEATEN PATH.

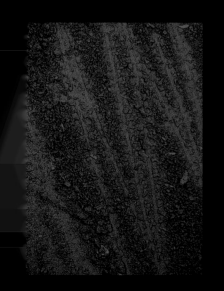

"This is no day camp," said Christy Rosen, a former director of the race. "These kids take their racing very seriously. They're out for blood."

Many successful BMX racers go on to make a name for themselves in other types of racing. John Tomac, an Olympic competitor, got his start as a BMXer. Roy Knickman, who rode for the 7-Eleven team in the Tour de France, also started out on BMX bikes.

Mountain bike racing was inspired in part by BMX racing. With their sturdy frames and wide tires that let riders go off the road and career over just about any kind of terrain, BMX

bikes are just fun to ride. It was enough to make adults jealous. Today, mountain bikers can choose from four types of races—cross-country, **obstacle course**, uphill, or downhill.

Cross-country races are the most physically challenging. Each race is a test of endurance, strength, and speed. Most cover a distance of 20 miles (32 km) and last for several hours. All riders start these races at the same time and pedal over an established course through mountains and rolling terrain. Juli Furtado, one of the most successful bicycle competitors of all time, was a cross-country racer.

OBSTACLE COURSE AND DOWN-HILL RACES TEST NOT ONLY THE SKILL AND BALANCE OF RIDERS, BUT THEIR COURAGE AS WELL.

obstacle course *a racing course or track including objects that must be jumped or avoided*

trials *bicycle races that test a particular skill, such as speed or handling*

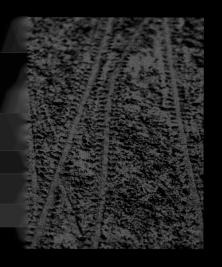

dab *touching one's foot to the ground while riding a bicycle in competition*

climbs *bicycle races that take riders up a hill or mountain*

Obstacle course races, or **trials**, are short competitions that test bike-handling skills. Cyclists must stay on their bikes while riding over obstacles such as logs, steep descents, and slippery hills. If they touch a foot to the ground for balance, it's called a **dab**; at the end of the race, the rider with the fewest dabs wins. In some cases, the time of the run is also a factor.

In 1927, Tullio Campagnolo's frozen fingers couldn't unlock a wheel wing nut on his bicycle. He later invented the quick-release, a simple mechanical solution that revolutionized bicycle riding by allowing riders to change their bike tires quickly.

Uphill races, or **climbs**, require a great deal of strength. During these races, competitors ride one at a time against the clock. A climb might be a short sprint up an impossible hill or an hour-long test of endurance up the side of a mountain.

Downhill races challenge the courage of the bravest competitors. One by one, riders head down steep hills, racing at full speed to get the fastest time. The courses are usually gravel roads or dirt tracks, and riders are often lucky to simply stay upright. Despite the likelihood of crashes, downhill racing has become very popular among mountain bikers.

The biggest mountain bike competition is the Mammoth Cycling Classic, held every year at Mammoth Mountain, California. This race is considered the official world championship, and the winner of the cross-country race at Mammoth is crowned the world champion of mountain biking.

Before 1911, bicycles had single gears or riders had to stop and get off their bikes in order to change gears manually. When manufacturers invented the derailleur, riders could change gears without having to stop.

Ned Overend was one of the first great mountain biking champions, winning the world championship at Mammoth four times between 1986 and 1990. Overend has since retired from mountain biking and now rides in other kinds of competition.

Touring, the kind of riding that Greg LeMond became famous for, is still the top bicycling sport around the world. Touring is just what the name implies—riding a bike to tour an area and see the scenery. Expert and professional **tourists** compete in several types of races.

Marathons became popular in the 1970s after John Marino, a former minor-league baseball player, biked across the United States in 10 and a half days. Marino's time shattered the old record for riding across the country.

Tour bike riders also compete in **track races** and **time trials**. During a track race, riders complete a specified number

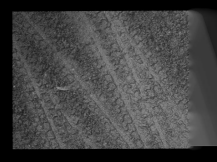

tourists *bicyclists who ride a touring bike*

marathons *long-distance tours that may cover an entire country or region*

track races *bicycle races in which riders must complete a certain number of laps around a track*

time trials *races to complete a short route in the least amount of time*

road races *bicycle races run on paved roads*

stages *sections of a long road race*

of laps around a track. They ride at top speed, so the turns must be steeply banked to keep them from flying off the course. In time trials, riders race against the clock to see who can cover a certain distance in the least amount of time.

The most popular form of touring by far is road racing. During these competitions, the roads are closed to automobile traffic, and spectators line the routes to watch racers cruise by. **Road races** may last an afternoon or many days. The Tour de France takes three weeks, but the riders don't stay on their bikes the whole time; they race in sections called **stages**. The winner is the rider with the best overall time.

Road races require strength of body and mind, because the longer races can be both physically and mentally exhausting. Riders must keep up their spirits and watch for opportunities to move ahead. Only those riders who know when to make the right move win major races.

Greg LeMond won his first world road championship at the age of 16. He later won it two more times, becoming the only American to have won the championship three times.

The biggest road race in the United States is the CoreStates USPRO Cycling Championship, held every year in Philadelphia. Riders cover 156 miles (251 km) by repeating a 14-mile (22.5 km) circuit. More than 300,000 spectators gather along the route to cheer on their favorite athletes.

The Tanqueray AIDS Rides, one of the newest cycling events, are held to raise money for AIDS patients. There are

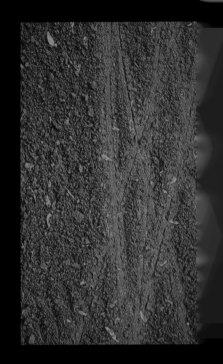

FOR ROAD RACERS, THE COUNTLESS HOURS OF TRAINING AND PREPARATION ALL PAY OFF AT THE FINISH LINE.

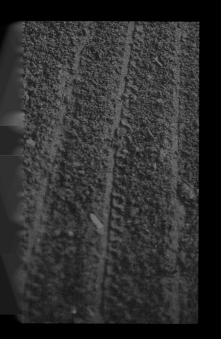

no winners or prizes, but the rides are high-profile events that help increase the popularity of bicycling.

Despite the growing interest in other biking competitions, the Tour de France is still the granddaddy of all road races. It is also the most popular annual sports event in the world, watched by more people than the Super Bowl. The yellow jersey awarded to the annual winner is the most prestigious trophy in all of cycling. Winning just one stage of the race can be enough to solidify a rider's career.

The Tour de France inspires all competitive bicycle riders to stretch their abilities to the limit. That's what bicycle racing—whenever and wherever it occurs—is all about.

INDEX